PSALMS
for SORROW

God's word for your journey through
the valley of the shadow of death

MAY HE WHO CREATES PEACE IN HIS CELESTIAL HEIGHTS, CREATE AN *abundance* OF PEACE FOR YOU.

ADAPTED FROM THE MOURNER'S KADDISH

Psalms for Sorrow: God's Word For Your Journey Through The Shadow of Death

Curated & interior design copyright by Tiye Chambers-Smith © 2020

Cover design by Ana Marinovic ©2020

ISBN 978-1-7335175-1-5 (pbk.)
ISBN 978-1-7335175-3-9 (ebook)
LCCN 2020901669

All rights reserved. No part of this publication may be reproduced, stored in a retrieval system, or transmitted, in any form or by any means, electronic, mechanical, photocopying, recording or otherwise, without permission in writing from the publisher.

Published in the United States by Aligned Press, Chantilly, VA.

Holy Bible, New Living Translation copyright 1996, 2004, 2007, 2015 by Tyndale House Foundation. Used by permission of Tyndale House Publishers, Inc. All rights reserved.

The Message Bible copyright 1993, 1994, 1995, 1996, 200, 2001, 2002. Used by permission of NavPress Publishing Group. All rights reserved.

The Holy Bible, The New International Version® NIV® Copyright© 1973, 1978, 1984, 2011 by Biblica, Inc.® Used by permission of Biblica, Inc.® All rights reserved worldwide.

IN THE VALLEY OF SORROW ...

" My soul is in DEEP ANGUISH.
How long, Lord, how long? "

Psalms 6:3

NIV

BUT MY SOUL WILL REMEMBER ...

" The Lord has *heard* my weeping. "

Psalms 6:8

NLT

IN THE VALLEY OF SORROW ...

" I AM WORN OUT FROM SOBBING. ALL NIGHT I FLOOD MY BED WITH WEEPING, DRENCHING IT WITH MY TEARS. MY VISION IS BLURRED BY GRIEF. "

Psalms 6:6-7

NLT

BUT MY SOUL WILL REMEMBER ...

" The Lord has *heard* my cry for mercy. The lord accepts my prayer. "

Psalms 6:9

NIV

" God, are you avoiding me? Where are you when I need you? "

Psalms 10:1

MSG

BUT MY SOUL WILL REMEMBER ...

" You, God, *see* the trouble of the afflicted; you consider their grief and take it in hand. "

Psalms 10:14

NIV

IN THE VALLEY OF SORROW ...

" How long must I wrestle with my thoughts and day after day have SORROW in my heart? "

Psalms 13:2
NIV

BUT MY SOUL WILL REMEMBER ...

" I TRUST IN YOUR *unfailing love*. I WILL REJOICE BECAUSE YOU HAVE RESCUED ME. I WILL SING TO THE LORD BECAUSE HE IS GOOD TO ME. "

Psalms 13:5,6

NLT

IN THE VALLEY OF SORROW ...

" My God, my God, why have you ABANDONED ME ? Why are you so far away when I groan for help? Every night I lift my voice, but I find no relief. "

Psalms 22:1-2

NLT

BUT MY SOUL WILL REMEMBER ...

" Yet you are holy, enthroned on the praises of Israel. Our ancestors trusted in You, and You *rescued* them. They cried out to You and were saved."

Psalms 22:3-5

NLT

IN THE VALLEY OF SORROW ...

"My life is POURED OUT like water, and all my bones are out of joint. My heart is like wax, melting within me. My strength has dried up like sunbaked clay."

Psalms 22:14-15

NLT

BUT MY SOUL WILL REMEMBER ...

" He has not ignored or belittled the suffering of the needy. He has not turned His back on them, but has *listened* to their cries for help."

Psalms 22:24

NLT

IN THE VALLEY OF SORROW ...

" Tears blur my eyes. My body and soul are WITHERING away. I am dying from grief; my years are shortened by sadness. "

Psalms 31:9-10
NLT

BUT MY SOUL WILL REMEMBER ...

" I trust in the Lord. For you have seen my troubles, and *you care* about the anguish of my soul. "

Psalms 31:6-7

NLT

IN THE VALLEY OF SORROW ...

"I AM WASTING AWAY FROM WITHIN. EVEN MY FRIENDS ARE AFRAID TO COME NEAR ME. I AM IGNORED AS IF I WERE DEAD, AS IF I WERE A BROKEN POT."

Psalms 31:10-12

NLT

BUT MY SOUL WILL REMEMBER ...

" He has shown me the wonders of His unfailing love. In panic I cried out. But you heard my cry for mercy and *answered* my call for help. "

Psalms 31:21-22

NLT

IN THE VALLEY OF SORROW ...

" ALL DAY LONG I WALK AROUND FILLED WITH GRIEF. I AM EXHAUSTED AND COMPLETELY CRUSHED. MY GROANS COME FROM AN ANGUISHED HEART. "

Psalms 38:6,8

NLT

BUT MY SOUL WILL REMEMBER ...

" You know what I long for, Lord; you *hear* my every sigh. "

Psalms 38:9

NLT

IN THE VALLEY OF SORROW...

"Day and night I have only tears for food. My heart is BREAKING as I remember how it used to be..."

Psalms 42:3-4

NLT

BUT MY SOUL WILL REMEMBER ...

" Now I am deeply discouraged, but I will *remember* You -- each day the Lord pours His unfailing love upon me. "

Psalms 42:6,8

NLT

IN THE VALLEY OF SORROW ...

"My thoughts trouble me and I am distraught. My heart is in anguish within me; the terrors of death have fallen on me. FEAR and trembling have beset me; horror has overwhelmed me."

Psalms 55:2, 4-5

NIV

BUT MY SOUL WILL REMEMBER ...

" Morning, noon, and night I cry out in my distress, and the Lord *hears* my voice. "

Psalms 55:17

NLT

IN THE VALLEY OF SORROW ...

" O GOD HAVE MERCY ON ME! "

Psalms 56:1

NLT

BUT MY SOUL WILL REMEMBER ...

" You keep track of all my sorrows. You have *collected* all my tears in Your bottle. You have recorded each one in Your book. "

Psalms 56:8-9

NLT

IN THE VALLEY OF SORROW ...

" I AM IN DEEP WATER, AND THE FLOODS OVERWHELM ME. I AM EXHAUSTED FROM CRYING FOR HELP; MY THROAT IS PARCHED. MY EYES ARE SWOLLEN WITH WEEPING, WAITING FOR MY GOD TO HELP ME."

Psalms 69:2-3

NLT

BUT MY SOUL WILL REMEMBER ...

" THE LORD *hears* THE CRIES OF THE NEEDY..."

Psalms 69:33

NLT

IN THE VALLEY OF SORROW ...

" YOU HAVE ALLOWED ME TO SUFFER MUCH HARDSHIP... "

Psalms 71:20

NLT

BUT MY SOUL WILL REMEMBER ...

" YOU WILL *restore* ME TO LIFE AGAIN AND LIFT ME UP FROM THE DEPTHS OF THE EARTH. "

Psalms 71:20

NLT

IN THE VALLEY OF SORROW ...

" ... EVERY MORNING BRINGS ME PAIN. THEN I REALIZED MY HEART WAS BITTER, AND I WAS ALL TORN UP INSIDE. "

Psalms 73:14,21

NLT

BUT MY SOUL WILL REMEMBER ...

"Yet I still belong to You; You hold my right hand. You *guide* me with your counsel, leading me to a glorious destiny."

Psalms 73:23

NLT

IN THE VALLEY OF SORROW ...

" You don't let me sleep. I am too DISTRESSED to even pray! I think of the good old days, when my nights were filled with joyful songs. I search my soul and ponder the difference now. "

Psalms 77:4-6

NLT

BUT MY SOUL WILL REMEMBER ...

" I said, 'This is my fate; the Most High has turned His hand against me.' But then I recall all You have done, O Lord; I remember Your *wonderful* deeds of long ago. They are constantly in my thoughts. I cannot stop thinking about Your mighty works. "

Psalms 77:10-12

NLT

IN THE VALLEY OF SORROW ...

" Terrors have paralyzed me. They swirl around me like floodwaters all day long. They have engulfed me completely. Darkness is my closest friend. "

Psalms 88:16-18

NLT

BUT MY SOUL WILL REMEMBER ...

" LORD, YOU ARE *the God* WHO SAVES ME... "

Psalms 88:1

NIV

IN THE VALLEY OF SORROW ...

" O Lord, HOW LONG will this go on? Lord, where is your unfailing love? "

Psalms 89:46,49

NLT

BUT MY SOUL WILL REMEMBER ...

" You said, 'But I will *never* stop loving him nor fail to keep my promise to him. No, I will not break my covenant; I will not take back a single word I said."

Psalms 89:33

NLT

IN THE VALLEY OF SORROW ...

" The floods have risen up, O Lord. The floods have roared like thunder; the floods have lifted their POUNDING waves. "

Psalms 93:3

NLT

BUT MY SOUL WILL REMEMBER ...

" Mightier than the violent raging of the seas, *mightier* than the breakers on the shore - the Lord above is mightier than these! "

Psalms 93:4

NLT

IN THE VALLEY OF SORROW ...

" I'M SLIPPING , I'M FALLING! "

Psalms 94:18

MSG

BUT MY SOUL WILL REMEMBER ...

" Your love, God, took hold and held me fast. When I was upset and beside myself, You *calmed* me down and cheered me up. "

Psalms 94:18-19

MSG

IN THE VALLEY OF SORROW ...

" My heart is SICK , withered like grass, and I have lost my appetite. Because of my groaning, I am reduced to skin and bones. I lie awake, lonely as a solitary bird on the roof. "

Psalms 102:4-5,7

NLT

BUT MY SOUL WILL REMEMBER ...

"He will *appear* in His glory. He will listen to the prayers of the destitute. He will not reject their pleas."

Psalms 102:16-17

NLT

IN THE VALLEY OF SORROW ...

" I'M AT THE END OF MY ROPE ... I'M FADING AWAY TO NOTHING. I'M WEAK... AND CAN HARDLY STAND. "

Psalms 109:21-23

MSG

BUT MY SOUL WILL REMEMBER...

" I will give repeated thanks to the Lord, *praising* Him to everyone. For He stands beside the needy, ready to save them... "

Psalms 109:30-31

NLT

IN THE VALLEY OF SORROW ...

" Please, Lord, save me! Let my soul be at rest again. I am deeply TROUBLED, Lord "

Psalms 116:4,7,10

NLT

BUT MY SOUL WILL REMEMBER ...

" The Lord *cares* deeply when His loved ones die. "

Psalms 116:15

NLT

IN THE VALLEY OF SORROW ...

"I WEEP WITH SORROW."

Psalms 119:28

NLT

BUT MY SOUL WILL REMEMBER ...

" YOU EXPAND MY *understanding*."

Psalms 119:32

NLT

IN THE VALLEY OF SORROW ...

" I HAVE SUFFERED MUCH, O LORD; RESTORE MY LIFE AGAIN AS YOU PROMISED."

Psalms 119:107

NLT

BUT MY SOUL WILL REMEMBER ...

" You are my *refuge* and my shield;
Your word is my source of hope. "

Psalms 119:114

NLT

IN THE VALLEY OF SORROW ...

" No one gives me a passing thought! Hear my cry, for I am very LOW."

Psalms 142:4,6

NLT

BUT MY SOUL WILL REMEMBER ...

"When I am overwhelmed, you alone *know* the way I should turn."

Psalms 142:3

NLT

IN THE VALLEY OF SORROW ...

"I AM LOSING ALL HOPE. COME QUICKLY, LORD, AND ANSWER ME ..."

Psalms 143:4,7

NLT

BUT MY SOUL WILL REMEMBER ...

"I AM *trusting* YOU. SHOW ME WHERE TO WALK, FOR I GIVE MYSELF TO YOU."

Psalms 143:8

NLT

IN THE VALLEY OF SORROW ...

"My DEPRESSION deepens. Don't turn away from me or I will die."

Psalms 143:7

NLT

BUT MY SOUL WILL REMEMBER ...

" I run to you to *hide* me. For you are my God. "

Psalms 143:9,10

NLT

" Now, may the Lord himself, the Lord of peace, pour into you His peace in every circumstance and in every possible way. The Lord's *tangible* presence be with you. "

2 Thessalonians 3:16

TPT

www.ingramcontent.com/pod-product-compliance
Lightning Source LLC
Chambersburg PA
CBHW041821040426
42453CB00005B/125